# ARE READY TO BUY A HOME.

# THE QUICK-START GUIDE FOR FIRST TIME HOMEBUYERS

BY,

## DR. SARITA MITCHELL

*"How do I find a Realtor®?"*

*"What if I have "bad credit"?"*

*"What if I need down-payment or closing cost assistance?"*

*"What if my Realtor® isn't helpful?"*

*"What if my Lender isn't helpful?"*

# Quick-Start Guide Overview
## By, Dr. Sarita Mitchell

*Welcome and Congratulations!*

*Congratulations on taking the first step towards homeownership! Thank you for trusting me to give you preliminary information to guide your home-buying process. This is a process that requires communication, commitment and consistency. Purchasing a home is a frightening and daunting task for many people, regardless of whether you have some knowledge of the process or if this entire thing is just a complete, mystical theory. Either way, I hope this Quick-Start Guide gives you just enough to get started!*

## Sections

I.   The Realtor
II.  Finances
III. The Lender
IV.  Homeownership Education- Being Prepared
V.   What Do You Want?

Disclaimer:

Although the author has made every effort to ensure that the information in this book was correct at publishing time, the author does not assume and hereby disclaim any liability to any party for any loss, damage or disruption caused by errors or omissions, whether such errors or omissions result from negligence, accident or any other cause. This book was developed based on the author's experience and their opinion of important information for first-time homebuyers.

*Communication*

*Ongoing communication with your Home Team of trusted professionals is key in this process. Everyone involved has a mutual goal and interest in making you a homeowner. Whether it is a financial interest, a social interest (i.e. one or more members of your Home Team is also a friend, family member, etc.) or any other kind of interest you can think of, the point is for everyone to see this to the end. Moreover, your Home Team has knowledge and experience of the process that you may not have. Regardless of whether you have friends or family members who purchased a home and they experienced "this" or "that", everyone's experience is different, everyone's situations (financial, etc.) are different and everyone's housing needs and wants are different. With that being said, you need to establish trust through ongoing communication with your Home Team for the smoothest process.*

# I.    THE REALTOR®

So, your best friend's sister is a Realtor® and you have to use her or else it'd be an abomination and they'd never speak to you again in life, right? Even if this is true, there is no problem working with a friend or family member as long as you clearly establish your needs and expectations for them. Familial relationships do not exonerate someone from meeting your needs. The relationship you establish with a Realtor® is still one where the Realtor® has a fiduciary responsibility to you, as their client. Your Realtor® works for you- do not forget that. Now, this doesn't mean you get to lack in *communication* or the responsibilities assigned to you. You should be expecting your Realtor® to do the following: be readily available to you, be able to answer or find the answer to your questions, constantly look for the perfect home to meet your needs, utilize their exclusive access to pre-marketed listings, and whatever else needs to be done to help you become a homeowner. So therefore, you are equally held accountable for communication of (including changes to) your finances, your housing status, your housing needs and adhering to the deadlines, guidelines and/or tasks your Realtor® may assign to you. They cannot do their job if you don't do yours.

Have you chosen a Realtor®? More than likely, you know a Realtor®; many times, you know multiple. Real estate is a commission-only business. Realtors® do not make money until *after* you close or have settlement on your home. Therefore, there are many Realtors® looking for new clients in order to keep their income consistent; after all, this is how they earn a living. With this is mind, you may encounter those whose only concern is to quickly sell you a home and not consider your need for guidance, comfort throughout the process and education. Therefore, you must do your due diligence when deciding on your Realtor®. The referral or pre-established relationship, alone, does not make them qualified to be the one to see you through this process. Here are some things to address with your potential Realtor® before you get started:

- My needs
  - Discuss your needs and see if your potential Realtor® is able to help you address these needs. No Realtor® is going to know the answer to every single question you pose, however, their willingness (or lack thereof) to find the answer or provide suggestions, referrals, etc. is indicative of their level of assistance during the homebuying process.
    - Financial needs- do you need help securing grant-provided downpayment/closing cost funds?
    - Do you have any credit concerns?
    - Housing needs- multi-family vs. single family vs. townhome vs. condo…are they able to discuss with you the potential positives and negatives of each?
- My budget
  - Be prepared to discuss your budget. Your potential Realtor® should have a general understanding of the homes available in your desired location and what you may be able to get for your money

- o Distressed Properties
  - Your potential Realtor® should have a general understanding of the positives and negatives of purchasing a distressed property (Foreclosures and Short Sales).
- o What is Buyer Agency?
  - Your potential Realtor® should explain to you the different types of buyer agency and the relationship the two of you would establish
- o Understanding Documents To Be Signed
  - You will sign many documents during this process. Ask your potential Realtor® how they will ensure you understand the documents you will sign.
- o My Expectations
  - Be open, honest and clear about your expectations of them

The aforementioned list of topics to discuss is not an exhaustive list. You may want to ask additional questions or address other topics before feeling comfortable with your Realtor®. However, the information you gain from the conversation will be very telling for both you and the potential Realtor®.

Once you have selected a Realtor®, here are some general rules:

☐ Remember, your Realtor® is not a salaried employee.

    o There is generally no allotment for gas, lunch or anything they may use their funds for as they help you along the process. Therefore, do not waste their time. Do not ask them to show you houses that you have no intention of purchasing. You can always visit Open Houses until you are ready to secure a Realtor® that specifically represents you.

    o Communicate if your needs or desires change. Again, no one wants to work for free and that is essentially what a Realtor® is doing until you settle on your new home. If you decide to wait, if you are scared, if you have questions- **tell** your Realtor®!

☐ Choose one Realtor®

    o Do not lead multiple Realtors® on. Realtors® have a code of ethics they must follow when working with clients, which includes prohibiting the solicitation of other Realtors'® clients.

    o If you want to work with multiple Realtors®, make sure you communicate this with those whom you are working.

    o Having multiple Realtors® can create an issue with procuring clause. Discuss this with your potential or existing Realtor®

- Communicate

    - Keep appointments and be on time- be considerate of your Realtor's® time. Remember, they are not salaried and you may not be their only client so their time is just as valuable as yours.

    - Answer when they call, text or email you. No one wants to feel as if they are chasing or bothering someone. Keep an open line of communication.

- Inform Other Realtors® That You're Taken

    - Do not call listing agents (the agents of properties in which you have interest). If you have a question about or want to see a property, talk to **your** agent/ Realtor®. Your Realtor® is the only one you should be talking to.

    - Inform Open House & New Construction real estate agents/ Realtors® that you have a Realtor® and are represented

*Commitment- a word that too many of us fear. To commit is to trust and obligate oneself to something. I'm sorry, but if you want to be a homeowner, you have to commit to the process. One way to do this is to create a self-imposed deadline before beginning the process. Establish the commitment and obligation to yourself in order to hold yourself accountable. Therefore, you're not committed to the process, the Realtor® or the home, rather, you're committed to yourself and the goal you have set. Commit to the deadlines and tasks that will make you successful. You will be a homeowner. Yes, you ARE ready to buy a home.*

## II.   FINANCES

You cannot purchase a home without your finances in order. Whether you intend to use cash, secure a mortgage or use a line of credit, the key word in "home-buying" is **buy**. You need to commit to having your finances in order.

The first person on your Home Team was your Realtor® and now you need the other half of this team, your mortgage lender. Part of the benefit of having a Realtor® is that they may be able to help you with this, as well. Many Realtors® have established relationships with various mortgage lenders based on previous deals they have done together and the different mortgage products banks offer. Banks are able to offer government-backed financing options, such as FHA loans, while also having the liberty of designing and offering their own mortgage products. Based on your needs, your Realtor® may direct you to one or several different banks to discuss the best option for you. Yes, you must shop for a mortgage in the same way you'd shop for the best deal for anything else.

When searching for a mortgage, consider:

- ☐ The bank's interest rates

- ☐ Bank Incentives
  - o i.e. If you have an account with them, is there any benefit such as a discounted rate?

- ☐ First Time Homebuyer Mortgages
  - o Many banks have first time homebuyer mortgages. Call a mortgage lender and ask for the details, then compare the various first time homebuyer mortgages across several banks and credit unions. Who has the best deal?

- ☐ FHA, FHA 203K, FHA 203B mortgages

- ☐ USDA & VA mortgages (100% financing loans)

- ☐ Conventional mortgage

- ☐ Renovation Loan
  - o Maybe a fixer upper is all you can afford in your budget, yet, you can't afford to actually "fix it up" after you buy it. Banks offer renovation loans that combine the purchase and renovation cost into one loan to make this a more realistic and viable option.

☐ New Construction

    o  If new construction may be the best option for your budget,
wants and needs, consider New Construction loans offered by
different banks. Usually, the New Construction site has their
own in-house lender, however, you should still research other
banks to see if their products may be better.

## Renting vs. Owning

Many people resort to renting because there is peace of mind with regards to
responsibility and not having to take the fearful step towards homeownership.
However, whether you rent or own, you are paying towards the benefit of
homeownership- even if it is not for your own benefit. What does this mean?
Whether your landlord has a mortgage or their property (the one in which you
live) is paid off, your monthly payment contributes to their advantage of
homeownership. If they have a mortgage, **you** are paying _their_ mortgage every
month, putting the excess cash/profit in their pocket (the difference between their
mortgage and your rent is their profit) and paying into the equity they are building
in their home. If their home is paid off, meaning they either purchased the home
in cash or a renter paid off their mortgage for them, you are putting cash in their
pocket and paying into the equity they are building in their home. So either way,
whether the mortgage is your landlord's or your own, <u>you are paying a mortgage</u>

<u>every month whether you rent or own</u>. That means even if you're renting, you're paying the principal, interest, property taxes and insurance (mortgage) on a property. Discuss these terms with your Lender.

Look at the chart below to see how much you pay in rent over the years.

*Could you have put this towards a mortgage or cash purchase of a home?*

| Renting Over the Years | | | |
|---|---|---|---|
| | 2yrs of Renting | 5yrs of Renting | 10yrs of Renting |
| $500/month | $12,000 | $30,000 | $60,000 |
| $1000/month | $24,000 | $60,000 | $120,000 |
| $1500/month | $36,000 | $90,000 | $180,000 |

So, how much of a mortgage can I afford?

Using the chart below, you can determine the monthly principal and interest payment based on the rate at the top. For example, a loan at $100,000 would be $477.42 at a 4% interest rate. Therefore, if you've been paying $500/month in rent, you'll want to stay at about a $100,000 budget.

Obviously, the better the interest rate=the lower the monthly payment. You can afford more of a home with a lower interest rate. This is all more of a reason to shop around for different mortgages. You want the best rate and the best

mortgage product.

## Principal and Interest Chart

| Interest Rate | 4% | 4.5% | 5% | 5.5% | 6% |
|---|---|---|---|---|---|
| $100,000 | $477.42 | $506.69 | $536.82 | $567.79 | $599.55 |
| $150,000 | $716.12 | $760.03 | $805.23 | $851.68 | $899.33 |
| $200,000 | $954.83 | $1,013.37 | $1,073.64 | $1,135.58 | $1,199.10 |
| $250,000 | $1,193.54 | $1,266.71 | $1,342.05 | $1,419.47 | $1,498.88 |
| $300,000 | $1,432.25 | $1,520.06 | $1,610.46 | $1,703.37 | $1,798.65 |
| $350,000 | $1,670.65 | $1,773.40 | $1,878.88 | $1,987.26 | $2,098.43 |
| $400,000 | $1,909.66 | $2,026.74 | $2,147.29 | $2,271.16 | $2,398.20 |
| $450,000 | $2,148.37 | $2,280.08 | $2,415.70 | $2,555.05 | $2,697.98 |
| $500,000 | $2,387.08 | $2,544.43 | $2,684.11 | $2,838.95 | $2,997.75 |
| $550,000 | $2,625.78 | $2,786.77 | $2,952.52 | $3,122.84 | $3,297.53 |
| $600,000 | $2,864.49 | $3,040.11 | $3,220.93 | $3,406.73 | $3,597.30 |
| $650,000 | $3,103.20 | $3,293.45 | $3,489.34 | $3,690.63 | $3,897.08 |
| $700,000 | $3,341.91 | $3,546.80 | $3,757.75 | $3,974.52 | $4,196.85 |
| $750,000 | $3,580.61 | $3,800.14 | $4,026.16 | $4,258.42 | $4,496.63 |
| $800,000 | $3,819.32 | $4,053.48 | $4,294.57 | $4,542.31 | $4,796.40 |
| $850,000 | $4,058.03 | $4,306.83 | $4,562.98 | $4,826.21 | $5,096.18 |
| $900,000 | $4,296.74 | $4,560.17 | $4,831.39 | $5,110.10 | $5,395.95 |
| $950,000 | $4,535.45 | $4,813.51 | $5,099.81 | $5,394.00 | $5,695.73 |
| $1,000,000 | $4,774.15 | $5,066.85 | $5,368.22 | $5,677.89 | $5,995.51 |

*Loan Amount*

## Figuring Out Finances?

## Follow the Chart to See Your Next Step

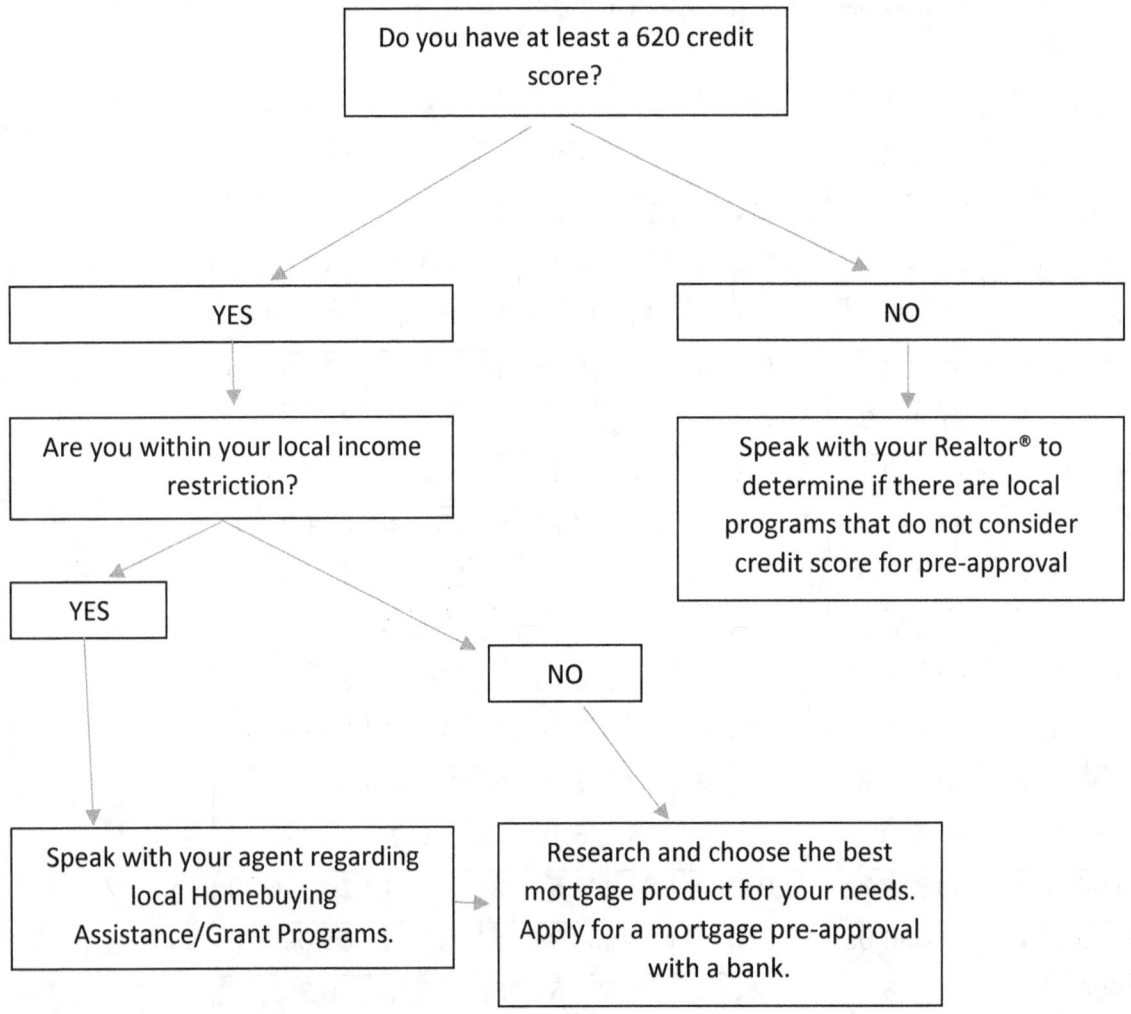

*Consistency*

*With regards to the homebuying process, consistency is established by your ongoing communication and commitment to the process. You will get tired. You will get frustrated. You may want to quit. Don't. Follow your deadline- you made a commitment to yourself that you will achieve. Trust in your Home Team and keep them informed of your feelings, your needs and your concerns. Be clear about what you want, where you want it and how much you want it for. Do not over exert yourself- your energy nor your finances. Stay on budget. Stay on the timeline. Stay on target towards the goal. Be consistent.*

## III. THE LENDER

As previously stated, the other half of your Home Team is your lender. Your Realtor® and your Mortgage Lender work in tandem to ensure you are successful in purchasing a home. They need each other. The Realtor® needs your finances to make sure your deal goes through. The Lender needs the Agreement of Sale, Contingencies and Settlement Company information from your Realtor® to ensure your settlement goes smoothly. They work together, behind the scenes (meaning, they coordinate much of the transaction between the two of them without much needed from you) to get the deal closed. Your Realtor® keeps everyone, including you, on task with regards to contractual deadlines, negotiates additional assistance (whether due to the inspection report, seller's [closing cost] assistance, etc.) and is the conductor when it comes to involving the necessary personnel to close on your home.

Your lender makes sure the most important thing is taken care of: the money.

Let's make this clear, though: if you are working with a lender and are pre-approved, you have demonstrated *commitment* and *consistency* to the homebuying process. Many people fall short when they're directed to a mortgage lender. They drag their feet when they are told to contact the mortgage lender, to provide them with the required documents (such as paystubs and W2s) and complete any other tasks to be pre-approved. Before you've even had a chance to see any homes (because many Realtors® will not show you a home unless you are pre-approved; it's a waste of time to see a home you're unsure you can even buy), you already have this daunting task of gathering all of this paperwork. Ugh. Frustrating, I know. But it needs to be done. Bottom line, you're not serious until you have a pre-approval.

Know this: you can always change Realtor® and/or Lender. Obviously converse with them, first. But just because one may refer the other doesn't mean you must stick with them if your needs aren't being met. Just make sure you discuss this with them and they are given the opportunity to change. You are the client and need the guidance, support and professionalism of their services. If you feel as though you are not satisfied with your Realtor's® or Lender's services, again, discuss this with them but know that you are able to move on if you desire. It doesn't matter if your Realtor® referred the Lender or vice versa, you owe no one anything if you are not properly being serviced. The conversation will determine whether it is a misunderstanding, miscommunication or if the actions are deliberate.

## The Mortgage Payment

The actual mortgage payment consists of the principal and interest. However, as a homeowner, you are also responsible for the property taxes and homeowner's insurance. Since property taxes and homeowner's insurance are annual expenses, homeowners have the choice of paying these two payments annually, quarterly or monthly. Discounts are typically offered for homeowner's insurance that is paid for at the annual rate (one-time payment). If you choose to divide one or both of these payments (property taxes and homeowner's insurance) throughout the year, this will be added to your monthly mortgage payment (principal and interest). Of course, all of these options are based on your finances and what works best for your budget. These options should be reviewed with both your Realtor® and lender.

Communication, Commitment and Consistency

*You've been openly communicating with your Home Team. You've committed to yourself, established a deadline and adhered to the ones given to you. You've been consistent with regards to your search and finances. If you are one that qualifies for a Homebuying Assistance Program, you will need to demonstrate these 3 Cs as you register and complete these programs to help you become a homeowner. There is plenty of help and money out there for the purpose of creating more homeowners. Homeownership strengthens communities, assists school districts and contributes to one's personal wealth. Here are quick overviews of programs that may be available to you based on your local municipality. Your Realtor® should be able to provide guidance here.*

# IV.  Homeownership Education- Being Prepared

A.  Homeownership Classes

a.  There are plenty local programs that offer **free** homebuying classes. <u>Take a class!</u> These classes are typically offered as a prerequisite to receiving homebuying assistance funds, however, they are open to anyone. The education received from these programs is invaluable.

i.  Why are they so helpful?

1.  The people running the programs have no "gain" in the process. They are neither the Realtor® nor the Lender and will give you unbiased advice.

2. I took one of these classes when I was searching

for my home and I learned more than I could ever

learn from my Realtor® or Lender.

b. The classes are typically only 1 or 2 days and lasts about 4-8hrs.

B. Homebuying Assistance Programs

a. **[Free]** Homeownership Classes

b. Provides Credit Counseling

c. May offer Home Repair Assistance for Homeowners

d. Downpayment/Closing Cost Assistance for first-time

homeowners that meet guidelines/restrictions

C. No/Low Credit Homebuying Programs

a. Requires:

i. Homebuying Class

ii. Credit & Homeownership Counseling

# V.   What Do You Want?

One thing you must be aware of is your Realtor's® inability to "steer" you. Steering refers to the practice in which a Realtor® attempts to steer clients to or away from a specific neighborhood, typically based on the clients' race. The Fair Housing Act more clearly defines this and other discriminatory housing practices by landlords, Realtors® and mortgage lenders. Take some time to familiarize yourself with the Fair Housing Act.

Due to the Fair Housing Act, your Realtor® should not steer you towards nor away from certain school districts, zip codes or neighborhoods. Therefore, you are responsible for determining where you want to live. Telling your Realtor® that you want to live in a "good area" or in a "good school district" inevitably puts them in a position in which they must steer you. The concept of "good" is determined by an individual/client and cannot be determined by your Realtor®. As a homebuyer, you must research areas and determine the best place to purchase a home. Remember that a home is an investment. Even if you think you may stay in your home forever, you must consider how much your home will appreciate in value, how you can build equity in your property and who you would be marketing your home to if you were to sell it in the future. Since the location of the home is the number one way to impact property value, here are some ways to determine the best location for you:

- ☐ School District

  - o Research local school districts. Many homebuyers begin their home search with a specific school district in mind. Even if the school district does not matter to you, it may matter to future homebuyers if you choose to sell. Homes in high-ranking school districts typically sell quickly, appreciate in value at a faster rate than lower performing school districts and are more coveted.

- ☐ Neighborhood Statistics

  - o If you are concerned about a "good area" or "safe neighborhood", you must do your own research to determine the statistics of specific areas and if you are comfortable with the results.

  - o Another option is to drive through the areas or developments that you are considering during different times of the day and week. This will give you an idea of the environment.

- ☐ Proximity to Recreational Activities

- o Maybe you enjoy being near malls, movie theaters, skating rinks, restaurants, etc. You may use this as means to determine which area is best for you.

☐ Public Transportation/Major Roads

- o If you need to be near public transportation or major roads, this will also help to narrow your search. Determine the area nearest the bus route, train station or major roads that you need.

Use the checklist below to determine what you want. Below is a starting point in determining what you want. Provide this checklist to your Realtor® and use it to establish *consistency*. Remember, you may need to compromise ☺

## Property Type

- ☐ Condo
- ☐ Townhome/Rowhome
- ☐ Single Home
- ☐ Multi-family Dwelling
- ☐ Mixed-use Building

## Budget

- ☐ _____

## Desired Location/School District

- ☐ _____
- ☐ _____
- ☐ _____

## Bedrooms

- ☐ 1 bedroom
- ☐ 2 bedrooms
- ☐ 3 bedrooms
- ☐ 4 bedrooms
- ☐ 5+ bedrooms

## Bathrooms

- ☐ 1 bathroom
- ☐ 1.5 bathrooms
- ☐ 2 bathrooms
- ☐ 2.5 bathrooms
- ☐ 3+ bathrooms

## Other Rooms

- ☐ Family Room
- ☐ Eat-in Kitchen
- ☐ Formal Dining Room
- ☐ Basement
- ☐ Loft
- ☐ Attic
- ☐ Garage

## Land

- ☐ 0-0.25 acres
- ☐ 0.25-0.50 acres
- ☐ 0.50-1.00 acres
- ☐ 1.00-1.50 acres
- ☐ 1.50-2.00 acres
- ☐ 2+ acres
- ☐ _____ acres

## Garage

- ☐ 1 car garage
- ☐ 2 car garage
- ☐ 3+ car garage

## Any Other Features

- ☐ Fireplace
- ☐ 2-story Family Room
- ☐ 2-story Foyer
- ☐ Central Air
- ☐ Forced Heat
- ☐ Gas Stove
- ☐ Master Bedroom ensuite
- ☐ Walk-in Closet
- ☐ _____
- ☐ _____
- ☐ _____

Thank you!

You have now reached the end of my Quick-Start Guide. I hope you have received valuable information to get you started with the homebuying process. There is more to learn from your Realtor® and Lender, as this guide serves to give basic information and guidance as you begin. If before reading this guide you were experiencing fear or confusion regarding *where to begin?*, I hope this guide has answered some questions and reassured you that:

Yes, you ARE ready to buy a home.

Sincerely,

Sarita Brown Mitchell, BS.Ed., MS.Ed., Ed.D, Realtor®

Licensed to Sell Real Estate in Pennsylvania

Contact: sbrown8m@msn.com for assistance with buying a home in Southeastern PA

Sarita has 9 years of experience in Education, including in administration and as an adjunct professor in Higher Education, in addition to 6 years in real estate. This combination of educating and leading adults and experience with various homebuyers has contributed to her knowledge and desire to assist first-time homebuyers.

Notes Pages:

Use these pages to take notes during your meetings with your Realtor®, lender and during Homebuying Workshops!

_____

_____

_____

_____

_____

_____

_____

_____

_____

_____

_____

_____

_____

_____

_____

_____

_____